Citrus Turtle Pattern

I0541317

Table of Contents

Large

Small

Medium

Citrus Turtle
Information

Tools
8mm crochet hook
Yarn Needle
Scissors
Stuffing Material

Safety Eye Sizes
Small: 12mm
Medium: 16mm
Large: 18mm

Abbreviations
CH: Chain
SC: Single Crochet
IN: Increase
DEC: Decrease
SL: Slip Stitch
BLO: Back Loop Only
FLO: Front Loop Only

Lemon Turtle

Buttercup

White

School Bus Yellow

Lime Turtle

Lemon Lime

White

Smoky Green

Orange Turtle

School Bus Yellow

White

Carrot Orange

Pink Lemon Turtle

Tan Pink

White

Pixie Pink

Citrus Turtle

colors I used

Lemon Turtle
Color 1: Bernat Baby Blanket in Buttercup
Color 2: Bernat Blanket in White
Color 3: Bernat Blanket Brights in School Bus Yellow

Lime Turtle
Color 1: Bernat Baby Blanket in Lemon Lime
Color 2: Bernat Blanket in White
Color 3: Bernat Blanket in Smoky Green

Orange Turtle
Color 1: Bernat Blanket Brights in School Bus Yellow
Color 2: Bernat Blanket in White
Color 3: Bernat Blanket Brights in Carrot Orange

Pink Lemon Turtle
Color 1: Bernat Blanket in Tan Pink
Color 2: Bernat Blanket in White
Color 3: Bernat Blanket Brights in Pixie Pink

Questions & Answers

Why do I start with a chain and end with a slip stitch?

Beginning with a chain creates a lift at the start of the row, leading to straight and even rows when a color change occurs

Do I have to use the recommended hook size and yarn?

You can use whatever hook size and yarn you would like. Different yarn weights require different hooks. Although Bernat recommends an 8mm hook, I personally prefer using a 6mm because I like to keep my tension loose. The thinner the yarn, the smaller hook size and vice versa.

8

Citrus Turtle

size small, shell

Color 1

8 sc in a magic ring
Row 1: CH 1, 8 IN, SL (16)
Row 2: CH 1, (1 SC, 1 IN)x8, SL (24)
Row 3-4: CH 1, 24 SC, SL (24)
cast off

Color 2

Row 5: 24 SC, SL
cast off

Color 3

Row 6: 24 SC in FLO, SL cast off

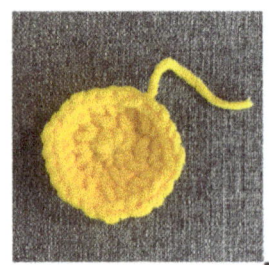

Citrus Turtle

size small, front fins

Color 1
8 sc in a magic ring
Row 1: CH 1, 8 IN, SL (16)
Row 2: CH 1, (1 SC, 1 IN)x8, SL (24)
cast off

Color 2
Row 3: 24 SL
cast off

Color 3
Row 4: fold flat, SL in BLO

SL back loops
together

with color 2, sew on lines

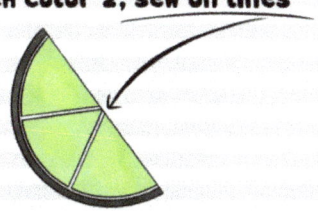

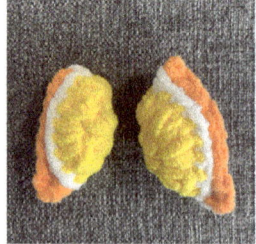

Citrus Turtle

size small, back fins

Color 1
8 sc in a magic ring
Row 1: CH 1, 8 IN, SL (16)
cast off

Color 2
Row 2: 24 SL
cast off

Color 3
Row 3: fold flat, SL in BLO

SL back loops together

with color 2, sew on lines

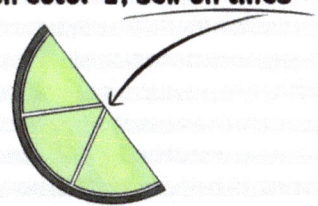

Citrus Turtle

*size small, head
and body*

Head in Color 3

8 sc in a magic ring
Row 1: CH 1, 8 IN, SL (16)
Row 2-3: CH 1, 16 SC, SL (16)
Row 4: CH 1, 8 DEC, SL (8) *attach the eyes!*
cast off

Body in Color 3

Row 1: 24 SC in shell BLO from
color 2 (white) row, SL (24)

Row 2: CH 1, 4 SC, attach front fin
into 2 SC, 4 SC, attach back fin
into 1 SC, 3 SC, attach back fin
into 1 SC, 4 SC, attach front fin
into 2 SC, 3 SC, SL (24)

Row 3: CH 1, (1 SC, 1 DEC)x8, SL (16)

Row 4: CH 1, 8 DEC, SL (8) *stuff!*

Cut & leave small tail, weave excess
yarn through stitch loops & pull to
close. Tie & pull excess yarn
through & cut

Citrus Turtle
size small, assembly

Stuff head and sew onto body

Using white yarn, sew on lines.
Follow the guide below.

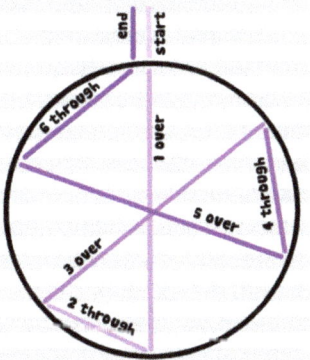

Tie and pull excess yarn through
body. Enjoy your finished turtle

Citrus Turtle

size medium, shell

Color 1

8 sc in a magic ring
Row 1: CH 1, 8 IN, SL (16)
Row 2: CH 1, (1 SC, 1 IN)x8, SL (24)
Row 3: CH 1, (2 SC, 1 IN)x8, SL (32)
Row 4: CH 1, (7 SC, 1 IN)x4, SL (36)
Row 5-7: CH 1, 36 SC, SL (36)
cast off

Color 2

Row 8: 36 SC, SL (36)
cast off

Color 3

Row 9: 36 SC in FLO, SL (36)
cast off

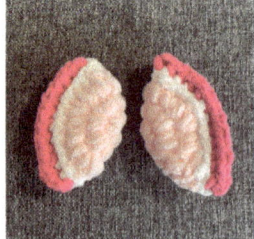

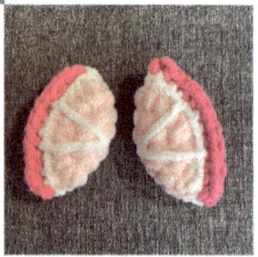

Citrus Turtle

size medium, front fins

Color 1

8 sc in a magic ring
Row 1: CH 1, 8 IN, SL (16)
Row 2: CH 1, (1 SC, 1 IN)x8, SL (24)
Row 3: CH 1, (2 SC, 1 IN)x8, SL (32)
cast off

Color 2

Row 4: 32 SL (24)
cast off

Color 3

Row 5: fold flat, SC in BLO

SC back loops together

with color 2, sew on lines

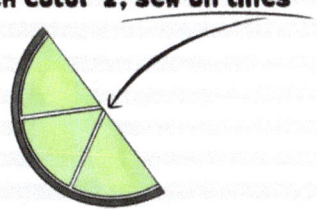

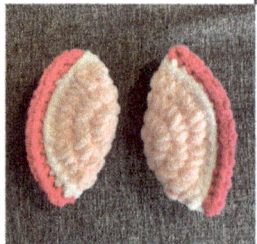

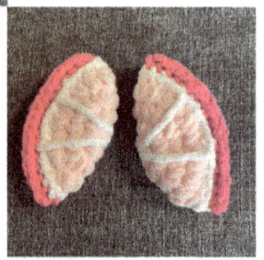

Citrus Turtle

size medium, back fins

Color 1

8 sc in a magic ring
Row 1: CH 1, 8 IN, SL (16)
Row 2: CH 1, (1 SC, 1 IN)x8, SL (24)
cast off

Color 2

Row 3: 24 SL (24)
cast off

Color 3

Row 4: fold flat, SC in BLO

SC back loops together

with color 2, sew on lines

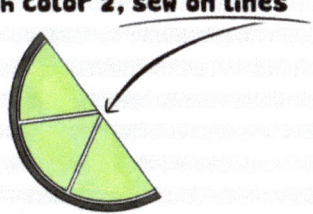

Citrus Turtle

size medium, head and body

Head in Color 3

8 sc in a magic ring
Row 1: CH 1, 8 IN, SL (16)
Row 2: CH 1, (1 SC, 1 IN)x8, SL (24)
Row 3: CH 1, (5 SC, 1 IN)x4, SL (28)
Row 4-5: CH 1, 28 SC, SL (28)
Row 6: CH 1, (5 SC, 1 DEC)x4, SL (24)
Row 7: CH 1, 12 DEC, SL (12) *attach the*
cast off *eyes!*

Body in Color 3

Row 1: 36 SC in shell BLO from color 2 (white) row, SL (36)

Row 2: CH 1, 5 SC, attach front fin into 3 SC, 5 SC, attach back fin into 2 SC, 7 SC, attach back fin into 2 SC, 5 SC, attach front fin into 3 SC, 4 SC, SL (36)

Row 3: CH 1, (7 SC, 1 DEC)x8, SL (32)
Row 4: CH 1, (2 SC, 1 DEC)x8, SL (24)
Row 5: CH 1, (1 SC, 1 DEC)x8, SL (16)
Row 6: CH 1, 8 DEC, SL (8)

stuff!

Cut & leave small tail, weave excess yarn through stitch loops & pull to close. Tie & pull excess yarn through & cut

25

Citrus Turtle
size medium, assembly

Stuff head and sew onto body

Using white yarn, sew on lines.
Follow the guide below.

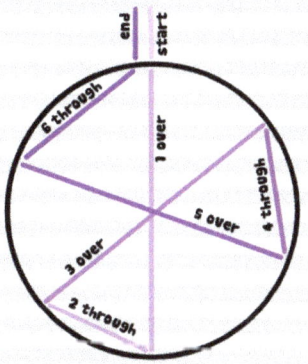

Tie and pull excess yarn through body. Enjoy your finished turtle

Want a tail?
4 SC in a magic ring
Row 1-2: CH 1, 4 SC, SL (4)
Cast off and attach the tail

28

Citrus Turtle

size large, shell

Color 1

8 SC in a magic ring
Row 1: CH 1, 8 IN, SL (16)
Row 2: CH 1, (1 SC, 1 IN)x8, SL (24)
Row 3: CH 1, (2 SC, 1 IN)x8, SL (32)
Row 4: CH 1, (3 SC, 1 IN)x8, SL (40)
Row 5: CH 1, (4 SC, 1 IN)x8, SL (48)
Row 6-8: CH 1, 48 SC, SL (48)
cast off

Color 2

Row 9: 48 SC, SL
cast off

Color 3

Row 10: 48 SC in front loop only, SL
cast off

Citrus Turtle

size large, back fins

Color 1

8 sc in a magic ring
Row 1: CH 1, 8 IN, SL (16)
Row 2: CH 1, (1 SC, 1 IN)x8, SL (24)
Row 3: CH 1, (2 SC, 1 IN)x8, SL (32)
cast off

Color 2

Row 4: 32 SL
cast off

Color 3

Row 5: fold fin in half, SC BLO
together across

SC back loops together

with color 2, sew on lines

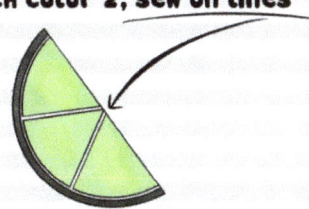

Citrus Turtle
size large, front fins

Color 1

8 sc in a magic ring
Row 1: CH 1, 8 IN, SL (16)
Row 2: CH 1, (1 SC, 1 IN)x8, SL (24)
Row 3: CH 1, (2 SC, 1 IN)x8, SL (32)
Row 4: CH 1, (3 SC, 1 IN)x8, SL (40)
cast off

Color 2

Row 5: 40 SL
cast off

Color 3

Row 6: fold fin in half, SC BLO together across

SC back loops together

with color 2, sew on lines

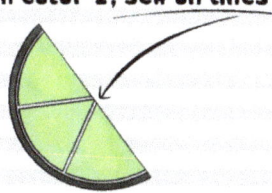

Citrus Turtle
size large, body

Color 1

Row 1: 48 SC in shell BLO from color 2 (white) row, SL (48)

Row 2: CH 1, 6 SC, attach front fin into 4 SC, 6 SC, attach back fin into 3 SC, 10 SC, attach back fin into 3 SC, , 6 SC, attach front fin into 4 SC, 6 SC, SL (48)

Row 3: CH 1, (4 SC, 1 DEC)x8, SL (40)
Row 4: CH 1, (3 SC, 1 DEC)x8, SL (32)
Row 5: CH 1, (2 SC, 1 DEC)x8, SL (24)
Row 6: CH 1, (1 SC, 1 DEC)x8, SL (16)
Row 7: CH 1, 8 DEC, SL (8)

stuff!

Cut and leave tail, weave excess yarn through stitch loops and pull to close, tie and pull excess yarn through and cut

Citrus Turtle
size large, head and tail

Head in Color 3

8 sc in a magic ring
Row 1: CH 1, 8 IN, SL (16)
Row 2: CH 1, (1 SC, 1 IN)x8, SL (24)
Row 3: CH 1, (2 SC, 1 IN)x8, SL (32)
Row 4-7: CH 1, 32 SC, SL (32)
Row 8: CH 1, (2 SC, 1 DEC)x8, SL (24)
Row 9: CH 1, (1 SC, 1 DEC)X8, SL (16)
cast off, leave long tail for sewing

attach the eyes!

Tail in Color 3

4 SC in a magic ring
Row 1: CH 1, 4 IN, SL (8)
Row 2-3: CH 1, 8 SC, SL (8)
cast off, leave long tail for sewing

Stuff head and tail then sew into place. Tie and pull excess yarn through

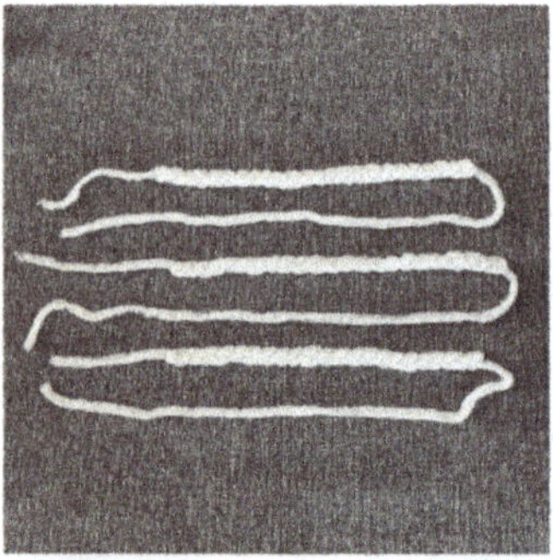

38

Citrus Turtle
size large, assembly

Add the Lines
Chain with color 2 until you have a chain the length of the shell, leave a tail as long as the chain. Use tail to sew on chained row. Repeat for other two lines across

Enjoy your finished turtle!

Share your results!

I would love to see your finished plushies!

Tag us please 🥰

You can tag either our business account, or my professional account so we can share your new turtle companion!

IG/Threads
@shop_simply_golden
@jasmin.deanda

YouTube
@stargazercreations

For Future Products

Want to see when new crochet kits are released?

Our kits are sold on www.simplygolden.shop

Follow our Instagram for updates @shop_simply_golden

Have a request for a kit? DM us or email us at simplygoldenretail@gmail.com

Love the kit and pattern? We would really appreciate it if you could leave us a review to help support our small business!

www.ingramcontent.com/pod-product-compliance
Lightning Source LLC
Chambersburg PA
CBHW051650120626
46551CB00015B/2295